Oprah Winfrey

An Oprah Winfrey Biography

Lotti Davidson

Table of Contents

#OPRAH2020

From rags to riches? Not an easy feat, but it has been done plenty of times before. When you're talking about someone like Oprah Winfrey though, you have to think bigger, and bolder.

How about… From poverty to the Presidency?

There has long been buzz around the multimedia mogul mounting a challenge against Republican Donald Trump for the United States Presidential elections of the year 2020.

Calls for her to run for the highest office in the land have come from various corners, particularly many Democrats, women, and people of color.

These calls include jokes, of course. But there is something about "#Oprah2020" that distinguishes it from other good-humored trending, celebrity presidential hashtags like "#TheRock2020" or "#Kanye2020" – that is, the scent of delectable, exhilarating *possibility*.

A black, female American from humble roots, with no experience in public office, whose main claim to fame and source of fortune is a long gone talk show, running to become the leader of the free world? It sounds like a pipe dream, yet Oprah somehow exudes a sense of credibility, and manages to carry such desperate hopes that it just seems possible.

She has repeatedly denied any serious interest in running for public office, much less the presidency of the most powerful country in the world. But the simple fact that #Oprah2020 keeps recurring in conversation and has staying power in the news cycles and the public imagination is phenomenal in itself.

It is proof of the heights she successfully scaled, even when she started from the very bottom.

This is the magic of Oprah Winfrey. She makes anything seem possible by her example.

Pop music's rebel superstar and cultural icon, Madonna once described herself as among the millions who have been inspired by Oprah, who "...*fights for things she believes in...*" even when some of her beliefs were unpopular.

Another music icon, Beyoncé, behind such empowering hits like *Single Ladies* and *Run the World (Girls),* expressed her admiration for what Oprah has been able to do for women specifically, crediting her for women's "...*new level of understanding*" of their possibilities as individuals.

This is a sentiment echoed by television media-mogul Shonda Rhimes, the storyteller impresario behind the addicting and long-running hits, *Grey's Anatomy* and *Scandal*. Oprah gave her an idea of what she could imagine and actualize for herself in media, for in seeing Oprah on television, she "... *saw something it had never occurred to me to imagine...*"

But then again, who could have imagined the heights climbed by Oprah Winfrey? She did not just have a talk show – it was one of the highest rating shows of all time, boasting of 25 years on the air and spawning careers and riches out of many people and objects who were featured there, as if everything she touched turned to gold. Beyond that, she was also a presence in print via the glossy *O* magazine, has a significant presence online, has her own television network, *OWN*, acts in television and film, produces movies and shows, and is a generous philanthropist and outspoken humanitarian.

In terms of dollars and cents, she is a multi-billionaire – among the top wealthiest African-Americans and blacks in the world. But in terms of political power and influence, consider this – she is widely credited for bringing a million votes to President Barack Obama when she endorsed his history-making run in 2007.

Oprah Winfrey: Black. Female. Winning in business and taking over the world. Inspiring others - people of all ages, races and sexual orientations - to do the same.

The late United States President, John Quincy Adams, was once quoted as saying, *"If your actions inspire others to dream more, learn more, do more and become more, you are a leader."*

It could have been a statement tailor-made for Oprah!

So from one leader to another… why shouldn't "The Queen of Talk" aim for the American presidency?

Introducing "Orpah"

One of the most famous names of all time, among the few that are recognizable even without a last name, is actually inaccurate to its owner.

Oprah Winfrey was actually born "Orpah," a biblical name from the Book of Ruth, particularly 'chapter 1, verse 14' as she would point out later in life. Spelling and pronunciation errors resulted in a swapping of the "r" and "p" however, and so we all ended up with the now-unforgettable "Oprah" instead.

A Difficult Childhood

Oprah Gail Winfrey was born on the 29th of January, 1954, in Kosciusko, Mississippi. Her unmarried parents had her quite young – her mother Vernita Lee was only 18 years old at the time and her father, Vernon Winfrey, 20. The relationship has been described as a "fling" and the couple never married.

Vernita left Mississippi to look for work, intending to move her daughter with her after she found a more sustainable situation for them. In the meantime, Oprah was left in Mississippi in the care of her grandmother, Hattie Mae Lee, who kept a farm.

Life in the rural community was not easy. They were said to be in such dire straits that there is a famous story of Oprah wearing clothes made of potato sacks.

But even with their difficulties, Hattie Mae Lee became an important influence on Oprah's life, and has been credited for her love of reading. It is her grandmother who taught her to read (as early as 3 years old by some accounts), beginning with the Bible. Oprah became so proficient she eventually had the ability to recite verses she had memorized and would do so before her grandmother's friends.

In this way, schooling came fairly easy for Oprah, which started with kindergarten at the age of 5. She was, after all, a quick study who already had a foundation in reading and writing.

When she was 6 years old, however, Hattie Mae became sick and Oprah was sent for by her mother. She moved to Milwaukee, Wisconsin to live with Vernita and half-sister Patricia in a boarding house.

Vernita did not have a lot of time to spare for Oprah; she was a maid with two children to support. She cleaned homes but sometimes had to rely on welfare for the three of them to live on.

Oprah moved homes again shortly afterwards. This time, she relocated to

Nashville, Tennessee – where her father, a coal miner and married by then, lived with his wife Zelma. Oprah was only 7 years old, but had already been in three homes.

Oprah's father Vernon and her stepmother Zelma had trouble conceiving their own children and were said to be eager to welcome the young girl. She had her own bedroom, and encouraging parents who nurtured her development by taking her to the library and church.

Family instabilities aside, Oprah did well academically. Enrolled then at Wharton Elementary School, she even skipped a grade.

Things, however, would change yet again. At the end of third grade, Vernon let his daughter visit Vernita in Milwaukee. This time, Vernita had an apartment with two bedrooms, one of which was for her children, who now counted three - Oprah and half-sister Patricia were joined by baby Jeffrey.

When Vernon returned to fetch Oprah and bring her back with him to Nashville, she is said to have chosen to stay back in Milwaukee with her mother and siblings. She began fourth grade there.

Instability within the family and constantly moving from place to place, however, turned out to be just one of the difficulties she would encounter in her young life.

At the age of 9, Oprah was sexually abused. The crime was allegedly done by a cousin who was supposed to be babysitting them while their mother was working. He is said to have raped her, then treated her out to ice cream and ordered her to keep the incident between them.

For a long time – a very long time – Oprah kept it a secret. Unfortunately, it was not the last such sexual abuse she would suffer in Milwaukee, or with people who were supposed to care for her. The years that followed saw abuse from family members including an uncle as well as a family friend.

She kept quiet about all of it throughout her youth and early career. She wouldn't even open about the topic until 1986, when she was already a successful woman with her own show.

Somehow, she still thrived in school. One of her Middle School teachers saw her love of reading and was instrumental in moving her to a different institution. She was able to attend Nicolet High School in Glendale, Wisconsin in 1968. Back then, she was said to be amongst the first few African-American students there.

It was an important time for civil rights in Milwaukee and the United States back then, so race relations weren't always easy. But as for her own experience, Oprah proved to be a popular student amongst her peers.

Unfortunately, she entered into a rebellious phase as a young teen. Whether it was part of growing up or because her mother was unable to give her enough time or guidance, or from the traumas she experienced and could not discuss - she started acting out.

She was dating, skipping school and had even run away and taken money from her mom. Vernita needed help, and Oprah needed direction. She was sent back to Nashville to live with her stricter dad.

But the troubled teen could not be spared from a particularly difficult situation – at the age of 14, she was already expecting her first child. The pregnancy was said to be the product of a promiscuity that emerged as a consequence of the abuses she had suffered. At the time, she was able to hide her pregnancy for months before she started showing unavoidable signs and had to tell her father.

She gave birth to a boy, but he wouldn't survive for more than two weeks.

Things changed when Oprah turned 16. In many ways, it was her love of reading that had saved her and turned her life around. The Maya Angelou-penned autobiography, *I Know Why the Caged Bird Sings* moved her so much that she read it several times and it changed her outlook in life. It was a book, she would later say, that "*validated my own existence.*"

Troubles aside, she always had a love of books, was a good student and a gifted public speaker. She found ways with which to move forward given her skill set. She was winning speaking competitions, and had even secured a college scholarship.

The Rise of a Media Superstar

From the time she was three reciting memorized biblical verses before her grandmother's friends, to the opportunities that came for public speaking along her time at church and school, it was clear that Oprah had a gift for speaking. She had talent – but she needed a platform to be heard.

This came in 1971 when she attended the White House Conference on Youth, as one of the students representing Tennessee. The radio station, WVOL requested an interview with her, which soon led to another chance to show her talent – at the Miss Fire Prevention beauty pageant.

She not only locked down the win, she was the first African-American to do so.

WVOL would be instrumental again in getting her voice to the public; they eventually gave her part-time work reading the news. She wasn't even a high school graduate yet, and two grades ahead of her peers too.

She finished high school at the age of 17 and continued working at the radio station. She then attended Tennessee State University under a scholarship. But her brains had beauty and charm to go with it too; she was also the winner of Miss Black Tennessee.

It was only onward and upward for Oprah Winfrey from there.

In 1973 at the age of 19 years old, she took a job with a local CBS affiliate in Nashville… that of an evening anchor. Thus did she become Nashville's youngest and first African-American female anchor.

But the demands of schooling and the broadcast journalism opportunities knocking on her door did not align. Oprah left Tennessee State University, just a requirement or two shy of graduating with a degree.

Her work next brought her to Baltimore, this time with an ABC news affiliate in Maryland. Again, she was a reporter and co-anchor on the news. She did not hold the job for very long, however. She had a more personal style that was not maximized to its full potential in neutral news that required objectivity. She got moved to *People Are Talking*, a daytime talk show, in 1977. This is the format where she really shined.

Oprah worked and lived in Baltimore for about eight years before relocating to Chicago in 1984. There, she was to helm the struggling daytime chat show, *AM Chicago*, which launched in 1983.

AM Chicago was pitted against the nationally-aired but Chicago-filmed talk show, *The Phil Donahue Show* and it was struggling.

With Oprah, *AM Chicago* successfully fought for better ratings and found success. It was eventually renamed after the host and called *The Oprah Winfrey Show* in 1985.

She was a shining star and hit-maker in Chicago, but it was only the beginning. Her work was being watched not only by plenty of Chicagoans but by eagle-eyed people who saw her gifts and believed they could propel her career to the next level.

One of them was acclaimed music producer and eventual "EGOT" winner Quincy Jones. "EGOT" stands for the very small number of people in the entertainment industry who could boast of awards in the Emmys, the Grammys, the Oscars, and the Tonys (his Oscar was an honorary one for his humanitarianism, but he had been nominated in competition many times).

In the mid-1980s, he wanted to give movie producing a shot. He got the rights to a book called *The Color Purple*. He convinced the visionary director Steven Spielberg to work on the film (at a staggeringly low price compared to his usual multi-million-dollar payday). What was missing though, was a cast with the acting chops to carry the burden of bringing the book's characters to life.

On a trip to Chicago, the producer switched on his television and spotted young Ms. Oprah Winfrey on *AM Chicago*. Jones once said it took him three days to find her name.

How could he or anyone else have ever predicated that just a few years later, the talk show host with the unconventional name would become so famous she could even be known just by a single letter – "O."

'Ho-ing' in Hollywood

Not content to conquer Chicago's airwaves in 1985, Oprah soon made her way to Hollywood.

Oprah's acting aspirations actually predate her desire to be a television host. She was once quoted as saying how she expressed her ambition to her father. But Vernon retorted something along the lines of 'no daughter of his' would be *"ho-ing herself."*

But venture into acting she did, and how.

Oprah had her acting debut in the film, *The Color Purple* (1985). As the story goes, she was spotted by Executive Producer, Quincy Jones in her stint hosting *AM Chicago*. He liked what he saw and felt she would make a great Sofia (a scene-stealing supporting character in the film), if she knew how to act.

In some ways Oprah was perhaps destined to become Sofia. One of the things that reportedly struck Quincy Jones about her was her unique name. Read backwards it spelled out "Harpo," which wasn't just a character in *The Color Purple*... he was Sofia's husband.

Was it a sign? Had confusion that changed Oprah's biblical name of "Orpah" all those years ago somehow contributed to her future success?

We cannot know, but at any rate her name was only the beginning. Oprah had to audition first, and winning the role meant more to her than just locking down a plum part in a Quincy Jones-produced, Spielberg-directed project...

Because even before she was engaged by anyone into the film, she already had a passion for the powerful, award-winning book it was based on.

The Color Purple by Alice Walker was published in 1982. It is the epic story of the life of Celie, a black woman living in the South in the early 20th century. *The Color Purple* follows her life for about forty years, as she and other African American women in her circle navigate the oppression of race and gender relations of the time period, until they each found their own version of peace.

It resonated with many African-American women, and especially so for Oprah. She is said to have finished it in one sitting, memorized lines from it, and even shared her love of the book to others by purchasing copies for co-workers.

Upon hearing news that a film adaptation was underway, she knew she had to be involved. She prayed for any kind of role in the project. And she meant *any - s*he even claimed she was amenable to helping people carry the script or bottles of water!

Thankfully, Quincy Jones had an eye for talent. It is said that he was in Chicago in connection with a lawsuit. He stepped out of the hotel shower and saw Oprah on TV. He then got in touch with top casting agent, Reuben Cannon. He told the agent he believed he had found the right woman to play Sofia.

The character is a sturdily-built, independent, outspoken woman. Oprah came in to read for the part, then had to cool her heels for months not hearing back from anyone on her performance.

But Oprah was never shy in pursuit of the things she wanted out of life. She broke from the usual Hollywood practice of 'don't call us, we'll call you' and rang the assigned agent.

She got a bit of an earful and hung up crying. She wept a lot. And in an early manifestation of the weight struggles that would famously follow her for years, she was somehow convinced her figure must have had something to do with being rejected.

Ever cognizant of making the next step forward, she resolved to pray and surrender her disappointment to God so that she could let go and move on. She also resolved to lose some weight by entering what was apparently referred to as a "fat farm."

It was at one such facility, during a rainy and tearful run on a track, that she got the call from Steven Spielberg.

Not only did he want to see her back in California... he also warned her losing weight meant she could lose the part!

Oprah left the facility and made sure to stop by a Dairy Queen for some ice cream before meeting with the famous director. They were in his office when he broke the big news – she was hired.

The Color Purple. The character of Sofia was a powerful figure of conviction and defiance… and Oprah Winfrey was a force of nature while playing her.

As Sofia, Oprah delivered some of the most powerful lines in the film, and a truly memorable one for many African-American women -

"All my life I had to fight…"

It was one heck of a debut; she was in a film adaptation of a Pulitzer Prize-winning novel by Alice Walker. It was a Steven Spielberg-directed film. She was part of a green but truly stellar ensemble cast, including a debuting Whoopi Goldberg on the brink of a Hollywood breakthrough, and Danny Glover who at the time only had a few credits to his name.

The film opened in December, 1985 and went on to gross over $142 million worldwide –

from a budget of $15 million! It was a commercial success and for the most part, a critical one as well - it was nominated for 11 Academy Awards.

For Oprah, the film was also impressive from a personal standpoint. Her performance as Sofia not only garnered great reviews, it even landed her an Oscar nomination for Best Supporting Actress.

The Oscars race for her category was intense. She was not only up against *The Color Purple* cast mate, Margaret Avery, she was also up against the talented Anjelica Huston for *Prizzi's Honor*, who eventually did end up bringing home the big prize.

Not that Oprah despaired too much about that outcome, if an account by her best friend TV show host, Gayle King, is to be believed.

Oprah had wardrobe issues in the hours leading up to the ceremony. Her Oscar dress

– and we all know how important the Academy Awards red carpet runway could be to a rising star's image – was problematic. The day before the awards it was too large and taken for adjustments. An hour before the awards and she found out it was returned to her altered too small.

Her dress therefore, made her so apprehensive about being called to the stage that she was said to be hoping they wouldn't call her name!

At any rate, the award went to the talented Anjelica Huston and it wouldn't be the only disappointment for *The Color Purple* along the course of what can easily be considered Hollywood's biggest night.

The Color Purple ended up losing in all the 11 categories it was nominated for. This gave the film a dubious Oscars record – alongside *The Turning Point* (1977), *The Color Purple* had the most Oscar nominations without winning a single one!

This outcome was ill-received by many in the African-American community… the NAACP chapter in Hollywood even filed a protest against the Academy.

But then again, commercial success and (general) critical acclaim aside, *The Color Purple* snub was perhaps just one more controversy in a project that had already faced many at that point.

Iconic African-American filmmaker Spike Lee (who started making waves in the industry in the 1980s) is a famous critic. Michelle Wallace, a black feminist, found issue with the dilution of the book's feminist message in sentimentality.

Some people found the movie's depiction of black men as unfair and possibly dangerous. They found it gave a disproportional amount of blame on them for the woes of black women, when black men are already being structurally held down by society. The movie has been described as racist but also dangerous because such a portrayal of black men could perpetuate unfair stereotypes and further racism.

There were protests at the premiere in Los Angeles. Heated discussions in community halls in Chicago and New York were organized, with passionate participants involved in heated discussions.

There was really so much debate around the film and how it depicted the power relationships between black men (shown as abusive) and black women (whose painful experiences were reflected in the movie).

But the film resonated amongst more people than those that it did not impress, and was especially touching to many black women. It *still* resonates now, in a world still marred by burden and constraint against women, especially those from the African-American community.

The film has shown lasting power and became so iconic it could be quoted by many women... including the music mega-star Beyoncé, who reportedly used some of its words in liner notes in an album. It also found life anew on the New York stage in the 2010s, with a slew of gifted young performers giving their take on the unforgettable characters. Among them was Oscar-winning actress and *American Idol* alum, Jennifer Hudson.

Unfinished Business

Oprah may have lost out in the Oscars, but it was clear that she had the chops and the presence to pursue this avenue of her media career. The next year, she appeared in the movie, *Native Son*. She would make and produce movies on and off from there.

During the filming of *The Color Purple*, work on *The Oprah Winfrey Show* did not stop. Oprah was filming the movie while filming her talk show in Chicago. It was picked up for syndication along the course of her work on *The Color Purple*, and her cast mate, Margaret Avery, recalled the producer Quincy Jones telling her his prediction that Oprah Winfrey was going to be a huge star.

But first, some unfinished business.

Oscar-nominated anchor of a hit Chicago daytime talk show is already a big achievement for most people, but Oprah was going to rewrite what success can mean for African-Americans and for women.

13 years after she left Tennessee State University shy of graduating, she had a nationally-syndicated talk show to her name

and an Academy Award nomination. TSU asked to have her as a speaker for commencement rites in 1987, but she wanted to finish her schooling properly first.

And so on these terms, Oprah did the work, submitted the papers and locked down her degree.

On Top of the World

The Oprah Winfrey Show was nationally syndicated in 1986. It was aired all across the United States on the 8th of September for the first time, and considered a big part of American pop culture history.

A Black Entertainer in Post-Racial America?

Oprah's rise to fame and fortune in the 1980s was part of a period in African-American history that has been likened to a 'Black Renaissance.'

It was a time marked by a surge in African-American cultural products and talents going mainstream, reaching a wider mixed-race audience across socio-economic classes, and receiving more credit and currency - often dominating the fields they entered.

Black Entertainment Television (BET) was launched in 1980; Michael Jackson's *Thriller*, which eventually became the bestselling music album in history, was released in 1982; Miss America crowned its first African-American winner with Vanessa Williams in 1983; *The Cosby Show* debuted in 1984, the same year Russell Simmons founded Def Jam Recordings and became one of the instrumental institutions in the wider acceptance of the rap genre; Mike Tyson was the youngest heavyweight world champ in 1986; and Michael Jordan was ruling college basketball and headed for the NBA.

Thus, the most celebrated cultural figures of the 1980s – Michael Jackson, Michael Jordan and Bill Cosby as mentioned above, plus Eddie Murphy for the movies and Whitney Houston for female pop music and of course, Oprah Winfrey for television – were all black.

The decade was not a particularly good time for African-Americans as a larger population – there was a widening wealth gap between the wealthy and the poor, the poor were getting poorer, and how the national economy was managed ultimately did little to help them. But culturally-speaking, black individuals were dominating the entertainment scene and setting representative examples for what could be possible given talent, grit, opportunity and of course, a little bit of luck.

For Oprah Winfrey, she was all but born with talent – intelligent and articulate seemingly from the get-go, she was skipping grades and speaking publicly from an early age. She had grit and courage to rise above the circumstances of her unstable and difficult childhood, with a dogged determination that would follow her all the rest of her life. She was given opportunities to rise, by people who spotted her blinding potential – from a grandmother who taught her how to read, to a teacher noticing her love of the written word, and a radio station that understood the early power of her voice.

She had a lot of luck too… Quincy Jones, it must be recalled, saw her on television during an unrelated trip to Chicago while stepping out of the shower. And she had captured his attention for casting in *The Color Purple* not only from what she displayed on screen… but also by her name, which was misspelled from original intent.

Oprah also had luck in terms of the historical context of the time in which she appeared across America. She was in many ways, the right woman at the right time.

Aside from a heady period of African-American talent bursting into the limelight in the mass media explosion of the 80s and the 90s, the years following the civil rights movement (whether rightly or wrongly) was also beginning to be enamored by the ideology of "colorblindness."

These years were becoming romanticized as "post-racial." In such a situation, overt and institutional elements of racism have supposedly receded, in favor of a broader ethos of sameness. This "sameness" highlighted individual potential and individual action toward success, rather than emphasizing on the need for structural and collective changes. Some critics say the ideology unfortunately became a detriment to true and effective racial reform.

The changes in the United States and the rise of successful African-American individuals have given conservatives a defense against further changes say, in affirmative action or electoral reform. An image of a post-racial America allows some to say, there is nothing to fix – just look at the rise of Oprah or, later, President Obama.

Whether or not Oprah Winfrey personally subscribed to the post-racial belief spreading in the time of her rise to national prominence, it had worked in her favor. She had broad, cross-cultural appeal.

"*I transcend race*," Oprah had once been quoted as saying and she had grounds to believe so – she attracted and retained a devoted following of both whites and blacks (not even counting viewers from other countries that eventually also aired her show).

She had also been quoted as saying race "*has never been an issue with me*" because it hadn't been a detriment to her path to success. Some scholars and social commenters noted statements like these made her a reassuring, "safe" figure who didn't alienate white audiences even as she proudly invoked her black legacy.

Whether she actively cultivated the image of being a "non-threatening" African-American cultural figure for the sake of a broader audience or due to personal belief and experience, we do not know. But the end result is the same – she courted and retained a racially diverse, mainstream mass following.

Oprah, as we now know, has since become more political. But at the time around when her newly syndicated show first aired nationally in 1986, part of her cross-cultural appeal grew from how well she played in the context she was in.

Oprah, after all, is a product of her history. That is, until she started making and shaping history herself.

From Employee to Business Owner

The Oprah Winfrey Show, carried on the wings of a gifted host turned Hollywood celebrity after her star-making turn in *The Color Purple*, quickly emerged on the top spot of daytime talk TV in the entire United States.

It was also critically acclaimed as soon as this winning bet burst from the gate.

It came out nationally in September, 1986 and by June the following year, *The Oprah Winfrey Show* was already raking it in at the Daytime Emmy Awards. In 1987, it took home statuettes for Outstanding Directing in a Talk/Service Show; Outstanding Talk / Service Show and – of course! – Outstanding Talk / Service Show Host.

Where most people could have happily stopped there, Oprah was only in her 30s and there is a reason why she sets imaginations on fire. She was ready and eager for more achievements under her belt.

She has been in the media industry since her late-teens, with experience on radio, television and even the big screen. Her *Oprah Winfrey Show* was a nationally-viewed, critical and commercial hit. She already had an Academy Award nomination. What was going to be next for Oprah?

How about Oprah Winfrey, media mogul? She was going to make the leap from network employee to bona fide business owner.

One of the biggest heroes behind the Oprah success story is her agent, Jeff Jacobs. He was a notoriously tenacious Chicago lawyer when she hired him as her agent in 1984.

Before Jacobs, she was doing quite well – as a popular Chicago TV host, she took the top spot from the previous king of talk, Phil

Donahue. She was paid $230,000 annually by the local ABC affiliate, WLS-TV, and her previous agent had locked in substantial salary hikes for the next few years.

She was reasonably satisfied, but as Oprah once told Forbes, her new agent "*took the ceiling off*" her thinking. And so with Jeff Jacobs on her corner, Oprah Winfrey went to work on taking her flourishing career to new heights.

First on the new agent's agenda was to retrieve the Oprah show's syndication rights, which were owned by the local ABC affiliate.

In 1985, ABC allowed Jacobs to bring the show into the independent market beyond Chicago, provided their stations in other cities could get first crack. It was in a sense, a no-lose situation for them anyway because federal rules placed restrictions on superstations like ABC relating to syndication. Jacobs then roped in a distributor, King World Productions.

In 1986, Oprah founded Harpo Productions, Inc. – "Harpo" is her name spelled backwards, as well as the name of her iconic *The Color Purple* character's husband. Sofia, it may be recalled, had once uttered the unforgettable line -

"...I loves Harpo. God knows I do. But I'll kill him dead before I let him beat me."

Oprah was the chairwoman and her unstoppable agent Jacobs, shared in ownership.

In the meantime, their distributor King World locked in big sales of the show and brought home considerable revenues in the two seasons that followed. Part of the profits went to Oprah and Jacobs.

Their success allowed them more leverage with which to bargain against WLS-TV, and

Jacobs soon went after ownership of the show on behalf of his client.

In 1988, they secured a deal with ABC and King World for the rights to *The Oprah Winfrey Show*. That same year, Harpo Productions, Inc. purchased a film studio in Chicago.

They took over production activities for Oprah's show and had greater freedoms on schedule and programming. They clearly knew what they were doing, too.

For after their Daytime Emmy wins of 1987, the accolades kept coming on an array of categories for more than two decades. The show also took in victories through the Critics' Choice Television Awards, the GLAAD Media Awards, the Image Awards, the People's Choice Awards, and TV Guide Awards.

But Oprah's critical wins also came alongside previously unimaginable commercial success. The distributor sold the show in several markets, which allowed them to take in a share of the distribution revenues. And the markets bid hard for *The Oprah Winfrey Show*.

This was because advertisers paid for spots on programs with ratings and Oprah not only brought in eyes and ears for her own show, her audience also tended to stick around for the channel's evening news.

Oprah had an almost halo effect on the news that followed her talk show, such that at the height of her show's ratings power, the news programs that came afterwards tended to be the highest rating in that market.

Speaking of this in terms of dollars and cents... a local station could bid up to six figures weekly just to be able to air *The Oprah Winfrey Show*. And in the mid-1990s, King

World could secure multi-year deals with 210 stations across the United States.

Aside from this revenue stream, Oprah also had other sources of wealth. In some later deals when her success proved phenomenal and hard to replicate, her Harpo Productions, Inc. and the distributor, King World, was even able to bargain with stations for a share in the ad revenues! Furthermore, she also got options on King World shares. Her show was also a hit overseas, where it aired in dozens of countries.

She also continued to act in and produce projects for television and film. Harpo Productions, Inc. had deals with ABC on airing their TV movies, and they also worked on theatrical releases.

In 1989, she took on acting again. Harpo Productions adapted the African-American novel, *The Women of Brewster Place* for television. She starred and produced in the miniseries, which had such a warm reception that it even spawned a TV series, *Brewster's Place* (short-lived though it was).

Harpo produced its first feature film, *Beloved*, in 1998. It was a film adaptation of the novel by Nobel laureate Toni Morrison, and was released by the Walt Disney Company. It wasn't a hit, but there were more film and TV projects in the pipeline.

The production company was especially talented in made-for-TV projects which drew in ratings, like *Before Women Had Wings*; *The Wedding*; and an adaptation of the book, *Tuesdays With Morrie*, which actually won four Emmy Awards.

All of these Oprah accomplished while working on *The Oprah Winfrey Show*, which continued to be relevant and successful. One of the great successes of her program was Oprah's Book Cub, launched in 1996.

In these monthly episodes, she would present a book that she liked and have the author on the show as a guest. This kind of priceless publicity and recommendation usually sent book sales through the roof… with an Oprah pick having the power to yield sales as high as a million copies.

It was clear that Oprah had not just a bankable name, but a veritable brand with a loyal following. She found many other opportunities to maximize it.

Oprah.com came out in 1998. In 2000, she launched *O, The Oprah Magazine*. She worked on it with Hearst Magazines, but had complete creative control. The result was a publication that was a version of her show, with similar, on-brand content. She had millions of subscribers and it yielded $1 billion in consumer revenue in 15 years. She wrote bestselling books. She has a podcast. She launched her own cable network, rightfully called OWN – The Oprah Winfrey

Network. It was on-brand and oriented to the female market, with one of its hits, *Queen Sugar*, bringing in millions of viewers.

She was also involved in other ventures, some of which used her name while others were part of her diverse investments. She had a wealth of real estate all over the United States. She had interests in the cable TV network, Oxygen. She was also a spokesperson for and had shares in the weight-loss company, Weight Watchers.

When she was only 32 years old, she hit the millionaire mark. By 2003, she was the first African-American female billionaire. She would grow that wealth again and again such that by 2018, Oprah Winfrey at the age of 63, had a net worth of almost $3 billion, grown over a stellar career of over 4 decades. She is widely considered to be one of the richest self-made people in the United States.

Her main source of wealth and fame, *The Oprah Winfrey Show* ran for 25 years, and was the highest-rated American talk show of all time. It was also amongst the most awarded, including of course, its superstar host.

She won for hosting in 1987; from 1991 to 1995; and again in 1998. She won her 7th Emmy Award and a lifetime achievement award in the ceremonies of 1999, and afterwards stopped submitting her work for contention (the show, however, still continued to submit for technical award categories honoring the work of the staff and crew). The rationale may be found in an interview, where she has been quoted as saying that following a lifetime achievement nod, *"what else is there?"*

Miss Winfrey indeed had other fish to fry. What was she to do with one more award as a show host when she already had several; when she already had a lifetime achievement award; and was an inductee into the

Academy of Television Arts & Sciences Hall of Fame prior to that? It was clear by the 1990s that she was more than a host and bigger than television.

She had a powerful voice, which she had long been using to go beyond her talk show and beyond entertainment to create a positive change in the world.

She brought her child protection advocacy to Washington in 1991, and testified at the United States Senate regarding **the Child Protection Act**. The goal was to have a national registry listing convicted child abusers. The law, eventually called **"Oprah Bill"** by many, was signed by then-President, Bill Clinton.

It was only one of many contributions that help make America – and the world – a better place. The more money, power and influence she amassed, the more she shared. She is known to be a generous donor to various causes, but is also gifted at establishing her own charity foundations and launching her own programs.

The Oprah Winfrey Leadership Academy Foundation was established as a fundraiser for **The Oprah Winfrey Leadership Academy For Girls** in South Africa. Launched in 2007, the academy was founded for the betterment of both individual students and through them, their nation. The goal was to break the poverty cycle and create future leaders.

The O Ambassadors is a combination of her previous **Angel Network** and **Free the Children**. An initiative launched in 2008, O Ambassadors encourage and empower students to make positive changes in the world through actions in their communities. While this may sound small – students acting in their own communities – the initiative has proven so empowering it has raised money not only for supplies but even for building schools.

The Angel Network that preceded O Ambassadors was launched ten years earlier in 1998 with a simple proposition – she asked her viewers to donate some of their change and a little bit of their time.

The result? $3.5 million initially, which yielded 150 scholarships and 15,000 volunteers for Habitat for Humanity! Over the course of the Angel Network's run, they raised over $80 million for charity, with Oprah covering for administrative costs.

Through this initiative, millions were donated to relief efforts during hurricanes Katrina and Rita… on top of Oprah's personal donation, reportedly in the vicinity of $10 million. Among the Angel Network's biggest achievements? 60 schools built in 13 countries.

The Oprah Winfrey Foundation is a private charity that gives out grants to nonprofits as chosen by the mega mogul herself. Her usual causes revolve around education, women and children.

The US Dream Academy is one of the causes close to Oprah's heart. It is an after-school mentoring program oriented towards at-risk youth. As one of its champions, she has donated a lot of money to the organization – in 2009, that amount was to the tune of $900,000.

By some estimates, Ms. Winfrey has already given over $400 million to educational causes. She's granted hundreds of scholarships to **Morehouse College**, and donated millions of dollars to **A Better Chance**, which aims to help students of color have better access to quality education. She has also donated to **Save the Children**.

Culture and the environment have also benefited from Oprah Winfrey's generosity and vision of a better world. She has donated to **the Green Belt Movement International**, which plants trees and engages with communities in Africa; and donated millions of dollars to **the Smithsonian's National Museum of African American History and Culture**, among many others.

The Iconic Oprah

The Best of Oprah: Must-Watch

It is amazing what one woman was able to do with a daytime talk show and her personal talents. But looking back now, her success was really unsurprising given the magnitude of the performances she was able to churn out.

- Not to be missed was her star-making turn as spunky Sofia in the 1985 film *The Color Purple* under the direction of Steven Spielberg. She was scene-stealing, spellbinding and earned an Academy Award nomination as Best Supporting Actress for her debut film.

But Oprah was even more impressive playing herself – insightful, sympathetic, intelligent, funny, charming, brave and visionary – which came out best in *The Oprah Winfrey Show*.

Sure, over the course of about 4,500 episodes and 25 years on the air at the top of daytime talk TV, *The Oprah Winfrey Show* had its share of generic genre fare. But when she conformed to genre she was excellent, and when she introduced something new, she clicked with audiences and was unparalleled by all the other competitors who tried to follow her lead. Here is but a small sampling of the best of must-see Oprah on television, doing what she does best:

- In an episode covering the issue of sexual abuse, she made her own **Sexual Abuse Revelations in 1986** during her show. She confessed to having been a victim when she was a child. It was a landmark moment for Oprah and for television. Soon, there would be sofa confessions and tell-all's on talk TV aplenty. But Oprah was the queen of executing it with signature candidness laced with sympathy, warmth, hope and sense of purpose.

- She made heads turn and eyes widen for **1988's "Diet Dreams Come True,"** when she memorably dragged out a red wagon carrying 67 pounds of animal fat to illustrate and bring to visceral reality how much weight she lost. It was one of her highest rated shows, and also considered to be the beginning of her public weight journey. Many women across America were able to readily sympathize – her weight struggles and continued quest for wellness and beauty while navigating body positivity tended to mirror their own.

- While some observers opined that the early Oprah was post-racial or transcended race, she was always proud of her heritage and covered the charged topic of race relations in America on her show.

Most notably: (1) she visited **Forsyth County, Georgia in 1987** for a tense episode in a place which then had a reputation for racism; (2) she tackled interracial relationships on the 25th anniversary of *Loving v. Virginia* in the **"I Hate Your Interracial Relationship" episode of 1992**; and (3) she was in Los Angeles to get a pulse of what people felt in the aftermath of the Los Angeles riots trailing **The Rodney King Verdict** later in the year.

- One of Oprah's favorite episodes of all-time was **November 1993's "Only Good News."** In this feel-good hour, it delivered just as the title promised, with stories that warmed the heart and deeds like babysitting and hiring a job applicant over at Harpo.

- Her largest TV audience came when the Queen of Talk sat down to chat with the King of Pop for primetime. **The Michael Jackson Interview of 1993** drew in 62 million viewers over 90 minutes, where the mysterious star who has been mum about his life for years, opened up to Oprah.

- It was not her last pop culture coup, or the last time a superstar would entrust her to handle their truths. **Ellen DeGeneres Came Out as a Lesbian to Oprah in 1997**.

The former stand-up comic and then-beloved sitcom star of *Ellen* had been fielding rumors about her sexuality for some time. It was already known amongst the people close to her and was an "open secret" in the industry. But with a landmark *Time* Magazine cover feature, she declared "*Yep, I'm Gay,*" in mid-April 1997.

Shortly afterwards, DeGeneres featured in a Diane Sawyer interview and addressed the issue. But on the afternoon of the 30th of April 1997, she discussed coming out with Oprah during *The Oprah Winfrey Show*.

Just hours after the talk show appearance, Ellen DeGeneres' fictional "Ellen" came out to "Oprah" too – "The Puppy Episode" of the 4th season of *Ellen* featured the fictional Ellen Morgan talking to her therapist, played by Oprah! The groundbreaking, history-making episode was viewed by an estimated 44 million people… making the Queen of Talk part of entertainment history yet again.

- **Oprah's Book Club** began in late-1996 as something really simple and organic – she wanted to have the opportunity to discuss a book that she loved with her audience. She would announce a title for everyone to read, then return to it in a later show for discussion.

Basically it is just like any other book club, except bigger in size as well as in scope. The authors would be in attendance, and sometimes the show was filmed with authors and readers in intimate settings like dinner or tea and at home in pajamas.

Oprah always did have a love of reading. She called books her friends, and was actually gifting and exchanging books with people she cared about all the time – a producer on her show included. This producer was credited with the idea of trying out the Book Club for the show. When Oprah announced the founding of the book club on air, she called it one of her favorite moments.

The first title in the club was *The Deep End of the Ocean*. They did it every month for years and churned a staggering amount of book sales. Publishers were agog. Authors became superstars.

Unfortunately, the regular Book Club ended in 2002. She looked back on that decision as being moved by what eventually became the chore of book selection. Picking a title and figuring out all the logistics of it ultimately deducted from the enjoyment she used to derive from the simple pleasure of reading. After ending the original iteration of the Book Club, she reinstated it only when she was especially moved by a work.

Oprah's Book Club was the ultimate embodiment of Oprah in many ways – the topics in the titles reflected her values and worldviews. But it was also one of the greatest illustrations of the power she wielded as an influencer. Whatever she touched turned into a bestseller – this was Oprah's "Midas touch."

- *"You get a car, you get a car, you get a car..."* exclaimed the unparalleled Queen of Talk in the unforgettable **Car Giveaway of 2004**, when she gave her 276-member audience a Pontiac car estimated to be about $28,000 each.

- **Oprah's Favorite Things** was a regular themed show wherein the Queen of Talk, just as the title promised, rounded up her favorite things – presenting their features, explaining why she loved them, and of course, sharing them!

Audience members on this hottest of all *Oprah* show tickets went home with armloads of goodies loved by the media mogul. Some gifts couldn't even be carried by hand, with past favorites including vacations and TVs.

The theme was actually inspired by pajamas that she loved so much she wasn't just gifting it to people she loved left and right, in a 1996 episode she also had everyone in her audience wear them as she spoke effusively about its properties.

From 1996 to 2010, she shared her favorite things around the holiday season, amid audience hysteria.

The theme sometimes courted criticism for encouraging materialism in the holidays, but that wouldn't tarnish the event for Oprah. Their participation in this theme was usually a surprise for the audience , and for the show's beloved host - it was a way to show people that something magical can happen when it is unexpected.

- **President Barack Obama and the First Lady Michelle Obama** sat down with the Queen of Talk in 2011, the first sitting president to feature on her show with his wife. And it is of no surprise that they would stop by – Oprah backed him in 2007 over Hilary Clinton in their battle for the Democratic presidential nomination,

and her influence is said to have
rallied voters to his cause.
Despite her contribution to the
Obamas' success, however, this
interview is notable for another reason
– Oprah was nervous!

With literally thousands of interviews
under her belt, she looked back on
only a handful of times she was
nervous and this was one of them. The
others were in interviews with Nelson
Mandela, Sidney Poitier and Michael
Jackson.

- **The Final Episode of 2011** was a star-
  studded affair that looked back on the
  show's history and paid tribute to its
  iconic host. The biggest stars of the
  day all made their homages to Oprah,

including Tom Cruise, Beyoncé, Madonna, Aretha Franklin and Tom Hanks.

- **Oprah's Acceptance Speech at the 2018 Golden Globe Awards.** In January 2018, Oprah Winfrey became the first black female recipient of the Cecil B. DeMille award at the Golden Globes. It was not just a highlight of the event, it was so rousing it reignited talks of her running for public office.

The Controversial Oprah

Over the course of a 40-year career and 25 of these years on the air of a daily daytime talk show, Oprah's had a string of hits and important contributions to bringing attention to certain people and issues. She was a positive influence in many (oh so many) respects, but she also has enough history for a string of misses and/or controversy.

- **Harpo Productions' Revolving Door.** In 1994, a former employee of Harpo Productions, Inc. spoke ill of the work environment and sued the company for back pay and severance. Publicist Colleen Raleigh quit after eight years on the payroll. The two years around Raleigh's exit actually saw about a dozen departures from Oprah-related employment. The case was quietly settled out of court.

- **The "Omerta" Around Oprah.** The Raleigh case marked one of the few instances that people who worked around Oprah actually spoke up about what goes on behind the scenes. Her close-knit, secretive world bound by silence, courts controversy in its own right.

Revelations about her – even those leaning toward positive - are notoriously difficult to release. Some journalists reportedly had a hard time finding takers for books about Oprah. The famous celebrity biographer (whose work tended toward the sensational), Kitty Kelley, met walls in many places she turned to both for information and publicity.

Oprah's publicity machine and legal protections were so tight it seemed she had the power to contain any story and control her image. Confidentiality agreements reportedly abound in everything Oprah – from the staff at Harpo right down to service providers like caterers and plumbers!

Few have ever dared to challenge the confidentiality agreement. While Oprah's personal desire to live and work as a private person is understandable, and her need to protect her name and image are necessary to her business, some observers lament the loss of information about one of the most fascinating people the world has ever known. Some even say this could be a challenge for first amendment laws.

- Speaking of the law… In 1998, Oprah was dragged into court by Texas cattle ranchers on charges around the **False Disparagement of Perishable Foods Products Act.** The case stemmed from a 1996 episode about tainted beef, mad cow disease, and Oprah's comment about not eating another hamburger.

The episode was thereafter blamed for a dip in cattle prices, hurting the business of ranchers.

It was a trying time for Oprah to have to face charges in Texas while fulfilling her commitments to film a daily show. Like the big boss and hard worker that she is, Oprah buckled down. She moved the entire outfit to Amarillo for the length of the trial, which allowed her to be both at court and later in the day, working on a set!

She fought for her right to speak her mind, took the stand and won – beating the ranchers on their home court. She also won hearts in communities in Texas.

- Oprah is trusted by the stars to handle their stories – Liz Taylor, Michael Jackson and Ellen DeGeneres, for example. But sometimes, control slips away from her and a star's actions are sometimes detrimental to themselves.

For example, things took an unfavorable turn for the previously untouchable Hollywood superstar **Tom Cruise in 2005** when he guested on the Oprah show. The usually cool actor was giddily jumping on her sofa, exuberant and wildly in love with his then-girlfriend, Katie Holmes. It was uncharacteristically off-the-wall.

The interview became viral, and dented the Hollywood superstar's previously stellar career. He has since bounced back amazingly (he is the one and only Tom Cruise, after all!), but the viral moment remains internet-immortal.

- Just as the celebrity confession has its hits and misses, the Book Club also has an unexpected controversy that became one of the most unforgettable Oprah episodes of all time.

She had previously featured *A Million Little Pieces* by James Frey, which returned to the bestseller lists after the Oprah pitch. Unfortunately for Frey, the veracity of the supposedly true and personal account of recovery from drug addiction came into question shortly afterwards. He thereafter found himself in the crosshairs opposite Oprah's couch for an interrogation and dressing down in the **James Frey Interview of 2006**.

Years later, Oprah looked back at that interview with some regret about how she handled the author's dishonesty and how she may have failed to recognize the humanity behind the mistakes of the man and let her ego affect her. She and Frey actually sat down together for another interview in 2011 for a more productive conversation.

- **Oprah vs. Science?** Oprah is a powerful influencer who has the platform to form the opinions of the public. Sometimes her power leads to the likes of President Barack Obama…

other times, they lead toward the problematic James Frey.

Thus, the so-called "Oprah effect" is a doubled-edged sword. This is even more apparent in the field of controversial - some say "crackpot" or "junk" – science.

In 2007, she featured the actress Jenny McCarthy, who expressed distrust of vaccinations due to links with autism. Skepticism of vaccinations have yielded disastrous effects in the United States since, with some researchers citing the rise of McCarthy as impactful to the phenomena... and the resulting return of some diseases that would have otherwise been preventable.

Oprah has also been criticized for giving a platform to the intense health and wellness regime of former television star Suzanne Sommers in 2009. Dozens of pills, estrogen lotions, vaginal injections and the like were discussed, to the dismay of many in the medical community who questioned Sommers' expertise and pointed to the dangers of her regime.

An Oprah-anointed expert, the telegenic Dr. Mehmet Oz who guested on her show often and eventually had his own hit show and media empire, also became an influential superstar in his own right.

Unfortunately, he was criticized by some of his peers for discussing sketchy or unproven pseudo-scientific remedies. Among his troubles? A letter from doctors questioning his place in the faculty at Columbia University; criticism on the British Medical Journal; and a 2014 summons to appear at a senate hearing on consumer protection, where he was taken to task by a senator for discussing a so-called "miracle" product that offered his sizeable audience "false hope." The Federal Trade Commission also found his show's research problematic in 2015.

Oprah is also criticized for giving a platform to the controversial Phil McGraw, who also ended up with his own hit show in 2002, *Dr. Phil*. Dr. Phil has since been hit for his questionable credentials, messy past and he and his team's controversial (many say exploitative or unethical) means of getting good stories for the show.

The Personal and the Public Oprah

For so public a figure, who is often regarded as an "open book" in the things that she believes and cares about, Oprah Winfrey has remarkably been able to keep mum about her personal life.

She lived perhaps in a different time – her rise in the late-1970s to the early-1980s came before the 24/7 news cycle of the 1990s and before the internet and social media took over the world in the 2000s. She was therefore, a woman able to keep a lot of secrets.

It was a skill she was perhaps used to, learned the hard way. It may be recalled that when she was a child, she was abused by a number of relatives and she stayed silent for decades.

The "omerta" or code of silence around her, as a few pundits have remarked, may also be a result of the loyalty she inspires in those in her circle, as well as the power she wields that compel those around her to stay silent.

Either way, while we have a woman open about her opinions, her aspirations, the things she loves and the things that touch her – the public is still always an arm's length away from the enigmatic woman herself. This is probably most palpable in the case of her personal life.

Finding Love in the Spotlight

Like many women in the public eye, Oprah's love life was always under a microscope. In her climb to the top, she'd broken barriers in age, race and gender but this was not enough for some people.

She was young for plenty of her achievements. She was groundbreaking as an African-American too. But as a woman, she was also getting on in age in a society and an industry that still prized youth and tended to pry into the personal affairs of females.

She was an achiever extraordinaire and yet – people speculated on her sexuality. People wondered if she was ever going to marry, or have children.

And if she still wanted all of these things who could possibly match up to the heights of this brilliant and successful woman?

One of the most-watched *Oprah* episodes of all time was 1989's **How Fame Affects a Relationship**… and the man in the hot seat, uniquely poised to answer that issue was none other than Oprah's boyfriend, Stedman Graham.

In 1989, their relationship was less than a handful of years old. As of this writing, the power couple have been together for more than 30 years. Over that course of time, Oprah's fame, fortune and influence has only grown exponentially. It could only be surmised 'how *mega* fame affects this relationship' though, because they are infamously private about their lives. There are, however, some information known about the couple.

Stedman Graham came from humble beginnings. He was the son of a house painter and grew up in a predominantly African-American community in New Jersey.

Stedman Graham was a graduate of Hardin-Simmons University in Abilene, Tex., which he attended on a basketball scholarship. He finished studies with a Bachelor of Science degree in Social Work.

While his game secured for him an education, it was apparently not enough to be drafted by the National Basketball Association after he graduated. Still, he managed to play and do well in the European basketball League in the 1970s. He later pursued further education, securing a Master's in Education from Ball State University in Muncie, Ind.

He was previously married to Glenda Graham in the 1970s. They had a daughter, Wendy, but eventually divorced. Stedman is said to have met Oprah in Chicago in 1986, during a charity event.

Being involved in charity work is apparently a common denominator for the pair – Stedman, a former college basketball player, founded a nonprofit organization called Athletes Against Drugs. It would later be revealed that he also had a passion for improving African-American communities and for creating opportunities for people to improve their lives.

The tall, trim and handsome Stedman was not an immediate hit, according to Oprah. He was a former athlete standing at six feet, six inches tall and well-dressed. People were skeptical about his character from how he looked – was he a jerk? Was he just trying to use her for something?

They were hounded by rumors of trouble, including cheating allegations (later retracted by the columnist who had written about it) in 1989.

The relationship forged on. By 1991, he was already keeping a toothbrush in her apartment, which was situated just a few blocks from Oprah's Chicago condominium. They eventually lived together, which was publicly confirmed by 1995.

They were engaged in 1992, with a simple proposal he made in their kitchen. Far less simple? The story made waves nationwide, and the couple made it to *People* magazine's November 22, 1992 cover with a bright, all-caps headline declaring, *"OPRAH'S ENGAGED!"* One of the bulleted subtitles to the story was about starting a family with the note, *"…but hey, what took so long?"*

If they only knew – almost thirty years later, the couple still have not wed (as far as it is known) and the reasons for this are unknown. They are still together though, and are apparently happy with their status, whatever it may be, for it is not known precisely what that may be… for Oprah has reportedly made it clear she wants no more inquiries about marriage.

Inescapably, Stedman has been referred in some corners as "Mr. Oprah." And who could blame them? Not a lot is publicly known about him aside from always standing by the well-loved media Queen. But he opened up to the *New York Times* in a 1997 profile called *"They Used to Call Me Oprah's Boyfriend'."*

Stedman Graham was much more than that. He was a corporate man with business dealings in both Chicago and New York, aside from being involved in passion projects. He had his own ideas, his own advocacies and his own busy calendar.

He founded and ran S. Graham & Associates, a management, marketing and consulting firm with specialization in sports. He was also president of Graham Gregory Bozell, a marketing firm. Over at George Washington University, he was involved in sports seminars and marketing as well. He co-wrote a semiautobiographical self-help book, *You Can Make It Happen: A Nine-Step Plan for Success*.

Even with his own credentials, achievements and busy schedule, however, it still wasn't all smooth-sailing being Oprah Winfrey's main man. He confessed to some insecurity that traced to his childhood, but ones he was able to overcome with help from her patience and their support and love for each other.

Fast forward to the 2010s, and with the couple still being together and apparently in a harmonious and loving relationship, people are wondering – why not get married?

Oprah was once quoted as saying Stedman had traditional views of a marriage. This might not align with their "*untraditional relationship*" and might have even been detrimental to the marriage they could have had.

So at the end of the day, whatever they have apparently works for them. Stedman escorted her proudly at the 2018 Golden Globes when she received her Cecil B. DeMille Award; a proud moment for them both.

Forging Friendships

As integral to Oprah's personal life as her relationship to Stedman Graham is the friendship that she has with journalist Gayle King. If everyone knows Stedman as Oprah's boyfriend, then everyone also knows her best friend, Gayle.

Oprah met Gayle in Baltimore in 1976, where both were working for a television station. Oprah was 22 and a news anchor while Gayle was 21 and a production assistant. They knew each other but became truly friendly one stormy winter evening when Oprah invited Gayle to stay over at her place. Oprah lent Gayle clothes – right down to clean underwear. They clicked in many ways, and a legendary friendship was born.

The next forty years saw them both succeeding in their professional endeavors, while maintaining their family-like closeness. We know Oprah's built a multi-billion-dollar empire. Gayle on the other hand, has a successful career on television. But through it all, they stayed in each other's lives. Gayle picked Oprah to be her children's godmother, and the two women are known to speak on the phone several times a day. Oprah was also there for Gayle when her marriage ended in a divorce.

With so much intimacy between the two friends, and Oprah's non-marriage to Stedman Graham, it is of no surprise that the two female friends have courted rumors of actually being a romantic couple. But they are both pretty relaxed about that rumor. Oprah once said she understood why people's thoughts drifted that way, because the kind of friendship that they have is rare and without cultural definition.

The two women always supported each other and always wanted the best for each other… even when one is so obviously more successful than the other. But for Gayle, being in the shadow of Oprah does not diminish her own accomplishments. She is a self-possessed woman, secure in her own achievements. And why shouldn't she be? She has shown to have a long and sustainable career in television, and has three Emmys in her own right!

They've been hit by rumors of being romantic partners. They've been hit with rumors of jealousy. Another thing that people could not help but wonder about is if Gayle is profiting from Oprah's friendship and generosity. But Oprah said Gayle never asked her for anything, not even "for a dime," and that they share a mutual respect from being friends who do not want "anything from you but you." It was for both women, a friendship between equals.

Complex Family Relationships

For all that Oprah Winfrey has in her life – talent, grit, a career that has yielded her fame and fortune, good friends and a loving and stable even if untraditional romantic relationship – Oprah, like many people, always had to deal with complex family relationships.

She came from a broken home. Her growing up years were marked by frequent moves. She was abused as a child by people her family had trusted. But the family complexities weren't just part of her distant past.

When she became a famous person, one of her relatives spilled a secret she tried to keep for so long – that of her teenage pregnancy.

A family member had made almost $20,000 selling the story to a tabloid in 1990. She considered this her first experience at betrayal.

At first she was inconsolable. But in true Oprah fashion, she found a way to deal with it candidly and productively. She eventually addressed the story. She expressed her shame as a youth. She expressed her fears. She expressed anxieties over being kicked out of school when she was student, and of the story denting her public image when she got older and was a public persona. She feared people would "*expel*" her from being part of their lives.

But eventually, she found the truth liberating, and the revelation gave her another point of connection with the struggles of many women.

The 1990 revelation wouldn't be the last of shocking revelations about Oprah. She found out she had a half-sister by her mother, a woman named Patricia Amanda Faye Lee. Patricia was put up for adoption by Vernita who just couldn't care for her anymore, when Oprah was 8 ears old and away living with her dad. Oprah and Patricia did not even meet until the 2000's, spurred by Patricia's earnest and discreet attempts at piecing together her past and connecting with family.

In another instance, a relative intimated to a biographer that Oprah's dad, Vernon Winfrey, may not even be her real, biological father! A family source even expressed doubts about Oprah's account of having been sexually abused. She had also been recently hit n the press for limited support and connection with Vernon.

Family relationships are hard enough. But in 2018, she was also dealt a loss that any normal family has to deal with – the death of her mom, Vernita.

Vernita Lee passed away in Milwaukee on Thanksgiving Day of 2018at the age of 83 years old.

A Living Legend

In 1964, Oprah Winfrey was a young girl from a broken family in a struggling household. She was tuned in to watch the actor Sidney Potier make history at the Academy Awards as the first black man to win the Best Actor nod.

She watched, enraptured by the meaning and possibilities presented by the actor's history-making triumph, even as her mother came home, *"bone tired from cleaning other people's houses."*

It was such a meaningful experience that she recounted the event when she accepted the Cecil B. DeMille Award at the 75th Golden Globe Awards in 2018 – the first black woman to be the recipient of the honor.

She was cognizant of the likelihood that there was a number of little girls watching her accept the award.

For a long time now, Oprah has had a searing self-awareness of her capabilities as an individual, the responsibilities that come with her power and wealth, and of the hope and possibilities she ignites in others. And this gift for possibility is particularly invaluable because somehow, in Oprah's person, she carries a connection with *everyone.*

One of the most interesting things about Oprah was her ability to juggle and bear the inherent contradictions of her public image. This champion of women and children have no children of her own. She is spiritual, but has no official church and openly appreciates material things. This warm, sympathetic voice is a billionaire A-lister with wealthy, A-lister friends. She is a public person who is relentlessly private in her personal affairs.

She is in short, a little bit of all of us, even the most different of us. And that perhaps is the secret of her connection, and her success. She has a mass appeal that carries with it, mass hope.

Whether or not her gifts and her guts bring her to the White House, or she will stay on our television screens is unknown. But what is known is that whichever venue she finds to connect with and enrich audiences, she will likely continue to excel in.

Printed in Great Britain
by Amazon

60565335R00061